the little black journal series
travel

the sophisticated adventurers' portable

BY VIRGINIA REYNOLDS

ILLUSTRATED BY KERREN BARBAS STECKLER

PETER PAUPER PRESS, INC.
WHITE PLAINS, NEW YORK

Pour mes amis de Paris

Designed by Heather Zschock

World Time Zone Map © 2009 David Lindroth Inc.

Illustrations copyright © 2009 Kerren Barbas Steckler

Copyright © 2009
Peter Pauper Press, Inc.
202 Mamaroneck Avenue
White Plains, NY 10601

ISBN 978-1-59359-671-2
Printed in Hong Kong
7 6

Visit us at www.peterpauper.com

the little black journal series

travel

the sophisticated
adventurers' portable

CONTENTS

introduction

*A traveler without
observation is a bird
without wings.*

—MOSLIH EDDIN SAADI

Get Up and Go!

Where do you want to go today? Do you feel like a quiet retreat in the woods or a whirlwind tour of 7 countries in 10 days? Whatever your fancy, don't dream it—do it. More important, *record it*. You'll take thousands of photos. You think you'll remember. But nothing can capture your impression of the moment like a jotted note. Long after the suitcases are returned to the attic, this journal will enable you to relive the moments of your journey in a way that photos cannot capture. You can feel like a sophisticated foreign correspondent as you take note of the details—so soon forgotten—that make your trip special and unique.

A handy reference as well, this journal includes places to record the personal information—including detailed itineraries, out-of-town contacts and medical information—you'll want at your fingertips. Clever and sensible travel tips, packing lists, and such essential international information as currencies and dialing codes keep you in the know. Address pages provide ample room for taking note of new contacts and memorable restaurants, and the inside back cover pocket adds convenience. Let this journal become your most trusted traveling companion.

vital statistics

*Our battered suitcases were
piled on the sidewalk again;
we had longer ways to go.
But no matter, the road is life.*

JACK KEROUAC

PERSONAL INFORMATION

PASSPORT NUMBER

DRIVER'S LICENSE NUMBER

LOST / STOLEN CARD HOTLINES

OUT-OF-TOWN CONTACTS

NAME

ADDRESS

PHONE NUMBERS

NAME

ADDRESS

PHONE NUMBERS

NAME

ADDRESS

PHONE NUMBERS

NAME

ADDRESS

PHONE NUMBERS

NAME

ADDRESS

PHONE NUMBERS

NAME

ADDRESS

PHONE NUMBERS

MEDICAL INFORMATION

PHYSICIAN

TELEPHONE

CONDITIONS

PRESCRIPTIONS/DOSAGE

travel tips

*When preparing to travel,
lay out all your clothes and all
your money. Then take half the
clothes and twice the money.*

SUSAN HELLER

PRE-TRIP CHECKLIST

☐ Hold newspaper and mail deliveries.

☐ Arrange for boarding of pets, or hire a pet-sitter. Keep the number handy when you travel.

☐ If traveling by car, arrange to have a pre-trip service. Your mechanic should check fluids, tires, tire pressure, and other important things.

☐ If traveling by air, arrange airport parking or transportation.

☐ Check passports—they should be current for six months or more. A valid passport is now required for U.S. citizens traveling to Canada and Mexico.

☐ Check for visa regulations in the countries to which you're traveling.

- [ ] Check for any immunization requirements, and follow up with your doctor.

- [ ] Ensure that you have sufficient prescription medicine for the duration of your trip.

- [ ] Check the weather at your destination.

- [ ] Purchase trip cancellation and additional medical insurance.

All the pathos and irony of leaving one's youth behind is thus implicit in every joyous moment of travel: one knows that the first joy can never be recovered, and the wise traveler learns not to repeat successes but tries new places all the time.

PAUL FUSSELL

A SAFE TRAVELER IS A HAPPY TRAVELER

- Type out important information such as passport number, flight information, home address and phone, destination address(es), etc., onto computer-generated business cards. Print out several and laminate. Keep copies in your luggage, glove compartment, etc. (and leave one at home) in case of emergency. You'll have all your necessary information right at your fingertips.

- Consider purchasing a suitcase in a wild or outlandish color. Your lime green bag will stand out among the thousands of black bags on the luggage carousel, and is less likely to be stolen.

- Rooms on the upper floors of hotels are the safest.

PACKING

- These days, it's wise to check with your airline regarding regulations on bag size, weight, etc. The TSA also regularly updates its website, *www.tsa.gov/travelers,* with its list of prohibited items.

- Always pack a handful of zip-lock bags in various sizes for storing wet items, toiletries, small souvenirs, etc. They take up almost no space and have dozens of uses.

- Fabric softener sheets will help keep your clothing smelling fresh.

- Pack a change of clothes in your carry-on in case of a lost-luggage disaster.

- Keep a cosmetic case filled with travel sizes of shampoo, lotion, and other toiletries packed at all times. When you're ready, you can just pick up and go rather than hunt down individual items.

- Shoes can be packed in plastic bags (store socks, panty hose, etc. inside the shoes), inside socks, or even in old pillowcases. This will protect your clothes and protect your shoes from being scratched.

- Always pack your medication in your carry-on bag. Make copies of your prescriptions. Keep one copy in your carry-on and another copy inside your checked luggage.

- A small battery-powered reading light can be a lifesaver. Your cell phone also makes a handy flashlight in an emergency. It will provide sufficient light to find your car keys or unlock a door.

- Include a soft duffel in your luggage to pack dirty clothes for the return trip.

- Baby wipes and hand sanitizer—don't leave home without 'em.

- Bungee cords, in varying lengths, are also incredibly useful—from temporarily securing a burst suitcase to serving as emergency clotheslines.

- Before you pack, strip down your suitcase! Pull off old claim checks and stickers.

- If traveling in a group, pool your resources: one hair dryer, one laptop, etc.

- Electricals: Depending on where you're traveling, you may need voltage converters and adapters to operate your small appliances. *www.kropla.com/electric* can tell you everything you need to know about the equipment you'll need to keep your electrical appliances working and safe.

- The Universal Packing List (*upl.codeq.info*) is a terrific online application that enables you to build a customized packing list, complete with reminders and tips, for any kind of excursion.

- With clothes, stick to a single color scheme. Add flair with fun accessories that won't take up too much room in your luggage—or buy them at your destination.

- Binoculars aren't just useful for viewing wildlife. Take them along to museums, cathedrals, and other sightseeing destinations so you'll be sure to catch every detail of the architecture and even the passersby.

- Consider mailing your dirty clothes home via postal or courier service. More room for goodies, and probably cheaper than an excess-weight charge from your airline.

We don't go anywhere.
Going somewhere is for squares.
We just go!

—MARLON BRANDO
as Johnny Strabler in
The Wild One (Film)

TIPS FOR SKY AND SEA

- You simply can't predict the climate inside an aircraft. Prepare yourself by dressing in layers and even packing an extra pair of socks in your carry-on.

- The pressurized air inside the plane is very dry. Be sure to keep yourself hydrated during flights. Avoid alcohol and caffeine; drink plenty of water before and during your flight. And don't forget the moisturizer!

- Don't carry wrapped gifts. Security personnel will expect you to unwrap them at checkpoints.

- If you plan on using your laptop computer in-flight, you will need a special adapter to plug it in.

- Pack some extra plastic or wire hangers when embarking on your cruise. Staterooms tend to be short on these.

- Take advantage of any discounts offered by the ship's spas or other on-board activities while the ship is in port and other passengers are on excursions.

- Lower decks are better for seasick-prone passengers. Study the layout of your cruise ship to choose the cabin that best suits your needs. Most cruise lines have their ship plans online.

TRAVELING WITH KIDS

- Pack each change of clothes individually in its own plastic bag so kids can just pull out an outfit and be ready for the day with minimal adult intervention.

- Pack non-messy snacks like granola bars, fruit, or pretzels for the airport and the flight, as airport food is typically expensive and unhealthy. Many airlines have cut back on in-flight food and drink, so you can't be reasonably assured of even a snack during your flight.

- Pack an organizer with small pockets (such as a shoe organizer) with toys and books and hang it over the seat back where kids can reach it easily. This trick works equally well on airplane, car, or train trips.

- Consider purchasing or renting an age-appropriate book on CD (or podcast) for restless travelers.

- Have kids participate in the planning of your trip. Allow them to choose one activity per day, or have them plan a whole day's activities.

- On road trips, keep an eye out for elementary schools. A few minutes' romp in the playground will refresh everyone.

- Carry a photo of your child, and have your child carry your photos and contact information in case you get separated. Give kids a photocopy of their passports in case they need it, while you hold onto the real one.

- Pick up the hotel's business card when you check in, and have each family member carry one. You can also present it to taxi drivers who may not speak English.

- Instead of a guided tour, consider taking a local bus ride. It can be a great way for the kids and adults alike to see a new city and maybe even meet a few locals.

REMEMBERING THE FOLKS BACK HOME

- When traveling in foreign countries, consider doing your gift shopping in the supermarket. Favorites such as chocolate and soap will look downright exotic, and carry a much lower price tag than their gift shop counterparts.

- Before you travel, pre-address envelopes or write out labels with the addresses of family and friends for easy mailing of postcards and letters. Local stamps also make interesting gifts for the stamp collector in your life.

- Usually, coins can't be exchanged. Give your loose foreign change to the kids on your gift list. They won't know—or care—that it's worth two cents.

You've been traveling around the world too much to find out anything about it.

ARTHUR BANNISTER,
character in *The Lady from Shanghai* (Film)

Smart Travel Tip:

The TSA (Transportation Security Administration) is a great source of up-to-the-minute information for travelers, including a section on average security checkpoint wait times by airport and time of day. Take a few minutes before you travel to check out their advice:

www.tsa.gov/travelers

trip itineraries

You define a good flight by negatives: you didn't get hijacked, you didn't crash, you didn't throw up, you weren't late, you weren't nauseated by the food. So you are grateful.

PAUL THEROUX

Destination(s)

Travel group contact info

Transportation

Carrier name & contact info

Departing from

Date/time

Arriving at

Date/time

· ·

Carrier name & contact info

Departing from

Date/time

Arriving at

Date/time

· ·

Carrier name & contact info

Departing from

Date/time

Arriving at

Date/time

CAR RENTAL AGENCY

Contact information

Reservation number

....

CAR RENTAL AGENCY

Contact information

Reservation number

....

ACCOMMODATIONS

PLACE

Contact info

Reservation number

....

PLACE

Contact info

Reservation number

....

PLACE

Contact info

Reservation number

DESTINATION(S)

TRAVEL GROUP CONTACT INFO

TRANSPORTATION

CARRIER NAME & CONTACT INFO

Departing from

Date/time

Arriving at

Date/time

· ·

CARRIER NAME & CONTACT INFO

Departing from

Date/time

Arriving at

Date/time

· ·

CARRIER NAME & CONTACT INFO

Departing from

Date/time

Arriving at

Date/time

CAR RENTAL AGENCY

Contact information

Reservation number

....

CAR RENTAL AGENCY

Contact information

Reservation number

....

ACCOMMODATIONS

PLACE

Contact info

Reservation number

....

PLACE

Contact info

Reservation number

....

PLACE

Contact info

Reservation number

Destination(s)

....

....

Travel group contact info

Transportation

Carrier name & contact info

Departing from

Date/time

Arriving at

Date/time

• •

Carrier name & contact info

Departing from

Date/time

Arriving at

Date/time

• •

Carrier name & contact info

Departing from

Date/time

Arriving at

Date/time

CAR RENTAL AGENCY

Contact information

Reservation number

. . . .

CAR RENTAL AGENCY

Contact information

Reservation number

. . . .

ACCOMMODATIONS

PLACE

Contact info

Reservation number

. . . .

PLACE

Contact info

Reservation number

. . . .

PLACE

Contact info

Reservation number

DESTINATION(S)

....

....

TRAVEL GROUP CONTACT INFO

TRANSPORTATION

CARRIER NAME & CONTACT INFO

Departing from

Date/time

Arriving at

Date/time

· ·

CARRIER NAME & CONTACT INFO

Departing from

Date/time

Arriving at

Date/time

· ·

CARRIER NAME & CONTACT INFO

Departing from

Date/time

Arriving at

Date/time

CAR RENTAL AGENCY

Contact information

Reservation number

• •

CAR RENTAL AGENCY

Contact information

Reservation number

• •

ACCOMMODATIONS

PLACE

Contact info

Reservation number

• •

PLACE

Contact info

Reservation number

• •

PLACE

Contact info

Reservation number

DESTINATION(S)

TRAVEL GROUP CONTACT INFO

TRANSPORTATION

CARRIER NAME & CONTACT INFO

Departing from

Date/time

Arriving at

Date/time

• •

CARRIER NAME & CONTACT INFO

Departing from

Date/time

Arriving at

Date/time

• •

CARRIER NAME & CONTACT INFO

Departing from

Date/time

Arriving at

Date/time

CAR RENTAL AGENCY

Contact information

Reservation number

· ·

CAR RENTAL AGENCY

Contact information

Reservation number

· ·

ACCOMMODATIONS

PLACE

Contact info

Reservation number

· ·

PLACE

Contact info

Reservation number

· ·

PLACE

Contact info

Reservation number

DESTINATION(S)

TRAVEL GROUP CONTACT INFO

TRANSPORTATION

CARRIER NAME & CONTACT INFO

Departing from

Date/time

Arriving at

Date/time

CARRIER NAME & CONTACT INFO

Departing from

Date/time

Arriving at

Date/time

CARRIER NAME & CONTACT INFO

Departing from

Date/time

Arriving at

Date/time

CAR RENTAL AGENCY

Contact information

Reservation number

. . . .

CAR RENTAL AGENCY

Contact information

Reservation number

. . . .

ACCOMMODATIONS

PLACE

Contact info

Reservation number

. . . .

PLACE

Contact info

Reservation number

. . . .

PLACE

Contact info

Reservation number

daily diary

*Unusual travel suggestions
are dancing lessons from God.*

KURT VONNEGUT

DATE

LOCATION

NOTES

....

....

....

....

....

....

WHERE I ATE: _____

....

....

....

FAVORITE MOMENT: _____

....

....

....

....

....

....

....

DATE

LOCATION

NOTES

_____

_____

_____

_____

_____

_____

WHERE I ATE: _____

_____

_____

_____

_____

FAVORITE MOMENT: _____

_____

_____

_____

_____

_____

_____

_____

DATE

LOCATION

NOTES

_____

_____

_____

_____

_____

_____

_____

WHERE I ATE:

_____

_____

_____

FAVORITE MOMENT:

_____

_____

_____

_____

_____

_____

_____

DATE

LOCATION

NOTES

WHERE I ATE: _____

FAVORITE MOMENT: _____

DATE

LOCATION

NOTES

WHERE I ATE:

FAVORITE MOMENT:

LOCATION

NOTES

_____

_____

_____

_____

_____

_____

WHERE I ATE: _____

_____

_____

_____

FAVORITE MOMENT: _____

_____

_____

_____

_____

_____

_____

DATE

LOCATION

NOTES

WHERE I ATE:

FAVORITE MOMENT:

DATE

LOCATION

NOTES

_____
_____
_____
_____
_____
_____
_____

WHERE I ATE: _____

_____
_____
_____

FAVORITE MOMENT: _____

_____
_____
_____
_____
_____
_____
_____

DATE

LOCATION

NOTES

WHERE I ATE:

FAVORITE MOMENT:

DATE

LOCATION

NOTES

WHERE I ATE:

FAVORITE MOMENT:

DATE

LOCATION

NOTES

WHERE I ATE:

FAVORITE MOMENT:

DATE

LOCATION

NOTES

WHERE I ATE:

FAVORITE MOMENT:

DATE

LOCATION

NOTES

WHERE I ATE:

FAVORITE MOMENT:

DATE

LOCATION

NOTES

WHERE I ATE:

FAVORITE MOMENT:

DATE

LOCATION

NOTES

WHERE I ATE:

FAVORITE MOMENT:

DATE

LOCATION

NOTES

WHERE I ATE:

FAVORITE MOMENT:

DATE

LOCATION

NOTES

WHERE I ATE:

FAVORITE MOMENT:

DATE

LOCATION

NOTES

WHERE I ATE:

FAVORITE MOMENT:

DATE

LOCATION

NOTES

<u>WHERE I ATE:</u>

<u>FAVORITE MOMENT:</u>

DATE

LOCATION

NOTES

WHERE I ATE:

FAVORITE MOMENT:

DATE

LOCATION

NOTES

WHERE I ATE: _____

FAVORITE MOMENT: _____

DATE

LOCATION

NOTES

WHERE I ATE:

FAVORITE MOMENT:

DATE

LOCATION

NOTES

WHERE I ATE:

FAVORITE MOMENT:

DATE

LOCATION

NOTES

WHERE I ATE:

FAVORITE MOMENT:

DATE

LOCATION

NOTES

WHERE I ATE:

FAVORITE MOMENT:

LOCATION

NOTES

WHERE I ATE:

FAVORITE MOMENT:

DATE

LOCATION

NOTES

WHERE I ATE:

FAVORITE MOMENT:

DATE

LOCATION

NOTES

_____

_____

_____

_____

_____

_____

_____

WHERE I ATE: _____

_____

_____

_____

FAVORITE MOMENT: _____

_____

_____

_____

_____

_____

_____

DATE

LOCATION

NOTES

WHERE I ATE:

FAVORITE MOMENT:

DATE

LOCATION

NOTES

WHERE I ATE:

FAVORITE MOMENT:

DATE

LOCATION

NOTES

<u>**WHERE I ATE:**</u>

<u>**FAVORITE MOMENT:**</u>

NOTES

WHERE I ATE: _____

FAVORITE MOMENT: _____

addresses

No one realizes how beautiful it is to travel until he comes home and rests his head on his old, familiar pillow.

LIN YUTANG

ADDRESSES

NAME

ADDRESS

PHONE NUMBERS

E-MAIL

NAME

ADDRESS

PHONE NUMBERS

E-MAIL

NAME

ADDRESS

PHONE NUMBERS

E-MAIL

NAME

ADDRESS

PHONE NUMBERS

E-MAIL

NAME

ADDRESS

PHONE NUMBERS

E-MAIL

NAME

ADDRESS

PHONE NUMBERS

E-MAIL

ADDRESSES

NAME

ADDRESS

PHONE NUMBERS

E-MAIL

NAME

ADDRESS

PHONE NUMBERS

E-MAIL

NAME

ADDRESS

PHONE NUMBERS

E-MAIL

NAME

ADDRESS

PHONE NUMBERS

E-MAIL

—·—·—·—·—·—·—·—·—·—·—·—·—·—·—·—·—·—·—·—

NAME

ADDRESS

PHONE NUMBERS

E-MAIL

—·—·—·—·—·—·—·—·—·—·—·—·—·—·—·—·—·—·—·—

NAME

ADDRESS

PHONE NUMBERS

E-MAIL

ADDRESSES

Name

Address

Phone numbers

E-mail

Name

Address

Phone numbers

E-mail

Name

Address

Phone numbers

E-mail

NAME

ADDRESS

PHONE NUMBERS

E-MAIL

— · — · — · — · — · — · — · — · — · — · — · — · — · — · — · —

NAME

ADDRESS

PHONE NUMBERS

E-MAIL

— · — · — · — · — · — · — · — · — · — · — · — · — · — · — · —

NAME

ADDRESS

PHONE NUMBERS

E-MAIL

ADDRESSES

NAME

ADDRESS

PHONE NUMBERS

E-MAIL

NAME

ADDRESS

PHONE NUMBERS

E-MAIL

NAME

ADDRESS

PHONE NUMBERS

E-MAIL

NAME

ADDRESS

PHONE NUMBERS

E-MAIL

— · — · — · — · — · — · — · — · — · — · — · — · — · — · — · — · —

NAME

ADDRESS

PHONE NUMBERS

E-MAIL

— · — · — · — · — · — · — · — · — · — · — · — · — · — · — · — · —

NAME

ADDRESS

PHONE NUMBERS

E-MAIL

ADDRESSES

NAME

ADDRESS

PHONE NUMBERS

E-MAIL

NAME

ADDRESS

PHONE NUMBERS

E-MAIL

NAME

ADDRESS

PHONE NUMBERS

E-MAIL

NAME

ADDRESS

PHONE NUMBERS

E-MAIL

- -

NAME

ADDRESS

PHONE NUMBERS

E-MAIL

- -

NAME

ADDRESS

PHONE NUMBERS

E-MAIL

ADDRESSES

Name

Address

Phone numbers

E-mail

Name

Address

Phone numbers

E-mail

Name

Address

Phone numbers

E-mail

NAME

ADDRESS

PHONE NUMBERS

E-MAIL

NAME

ADDRESS

PHONE NUMBERS

E-MAIL

NAME

ADDRESS

PHONE NUMBERS

E-MAIL

ADDRESSES

NAME

ADDRESS

PHONE NUMBERS

E-MAIL

NAME

ADDRESS

PHONE NUMBERS

E-MAIL

NAME

ADDRESS

PHONE NUMBERS

E-MAIL

NAME

ADDRESS

PHONE NUMBERS

E-MAIL

--- --- --- --- --- --- --- --- --- --- ---

NAME

ADDRESS

PHONE NUMBERS

E-MAIL

--- --- --- --- --- --- --- --- --- --- ---

NAME

ADDRESS

PHONE NUMBERS

E-MAIL

ADDRESSES

Name

Address

Phone numbers

E-mail

Name

Address

Phone numbers

E-mail

Name

Address

Phone numbers

E-mail

official jet-setters' guide

INTERNATIONAL TRAVEL REFERENCE PAGES

*One's destination is never
a place but rather a new way
of looking at things.*

HENRY MILLER

TIME ZONES AROUND THE WORLD

Greenwich Mean Time (GMT), the time zone defined by the Prime Meridian o zero longitude—straddled by Greenwich England—is the starting point of the world's tim zones.

Generally, each time zone east of GMT is an hou later; each time zone west is an hour earlier (althoug exceptions can be noted on the fold-out map and i locations that do not observe Daylight Saving Time) When crossing the International Date Line—rough ly 180° longitude and opposite the Prim Meridian—you gain a day heading east, and lose day heading west. The International Date Line sepa rates the Eastern and Western Hemispheres in th Pacific. The date in the Eastern Hemisphere is alway one day ahead of the date in the Wester Hemisphere.

For the most up to date information, consult
www.worldtimezone.net

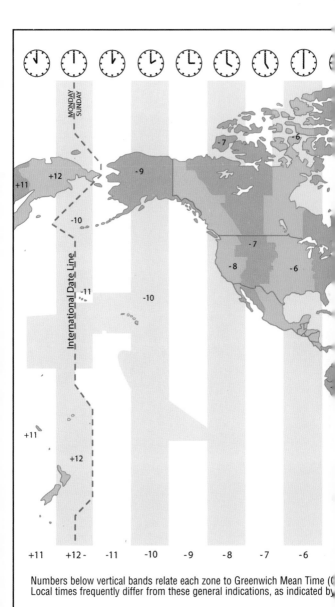

MONDAY
SUNDAY

International Date Line

+11 +12

-10

-11

-10

-7 -6

-9

-7

-8 -6

+11

+12

+11 +12 - -11 -10 -9 -8 -7 -6

Numbers below vertical bands relate each zone to Greenwich Mean Time (
Local times frequently differ from these general indications, as indicated by

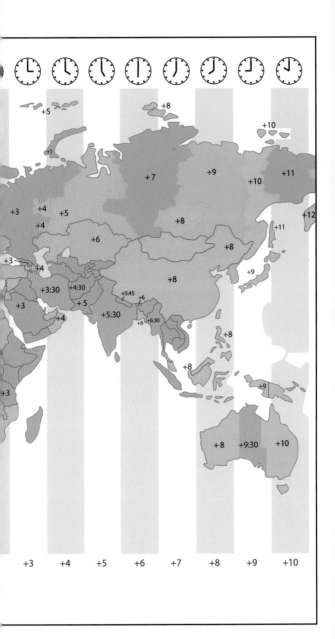

(hrs.).

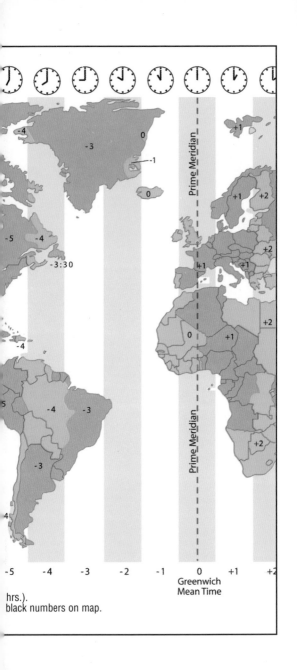

hrs.).
black numbers on map.

WORLD CURRENCIES

Many Caribbean countries have their own national currencies but also accept the U.S. dollar. Some European countries continue to maintain their national currencies while accepting euros. Many island territories in the Caribbean, Pacific, and Indian Ocean administered by European countries trade in euros. You can check exchange rates for every currency in the world at *www.xe.com.*

COUNTRIES THAT USE THE €

ANDORRA	IRELAND
AUSTRIA	ITALY
AZORES	LUXEMBOURG
BELGIUM	MALTA
CYPRUS	MONACO
FINLAND	NETHERLANDS
FRANCE	PORTUGAL
GERMANY	SLOVENIA
GREECE	SPAIN

SMALL TRAVEL TIP: Traveling with credit cards is easy—some might say too easy. Check with your bank before you travel to discuss any fees that might be charged when using your card away from home, especially if you are

COUNTRY	CURRENCY
ARGENTINA	*Argentine peso*
AUSTRALIA	*Australian dollar*
BOTSWANA	*Pula*
BRAZIL	*Real*
CANADA	*Canadian dollar*
CHINA	*Renminbi*
CZECH REPUBLIC	*Koruna*
DENMARK	*Danish krone*
EGYPT	*Egyptian pound*
HONG KONG	*Hong Kong dollar*
INDIA	*Indian rupee*
ISRAEL	*New shekel*
JAMAICA	*Jamaican dollar*
JAPAN	*Yen*
KENYA	*Kenyan shilling*
KOREA	*Won*
MEXICO	*Peso*

traveling to a foreign country, and notify them of your itinerary. Bank security departments are always on the lookout for unusual spending patterns, and may even freeze your account, especially if they can't contact you.

COUNTRY	CURRENCY
MOROCCO	Dirham
NEW ZEALAND	New Zealand dollar
NORWAY	Norwegian krone
PAKISTAN	Pakistani rupee
ROMANIA	Leu
RUSSIA	Ruble
SAUDI ARABIA	Riyal
SINGAPORE	Singapore dollar
SOUTH AFRICA	Rand
SWEDEN	Krona
SWITZERLAND	Swiss franc
TAIWAN	New Taiwan dollar
THAILAND	Baht
TRINIDAD & TOBAGO	Trinidad & Tobago dollar
TURKEY	New lira
UNITED KINGDOM	British pound
UNITED STATES	U. S. dollar

INTERNATIONAL DIALING CODES

To make an international call, dial the **Out Code** of the country you're calling from, then the **In Code** of the country you're calling.

COUNTRY	DIAL IN	DIAL OUT
Afghanistan	93	00
Argentina	54	00
Australia	61	0011
Austria	43	00
Belgium	32	00
Brazil	55	0014
Canada	1	011
China	86	00
Costa Rica	506	00
Czech Rep.	420	00
Denmark	45	00
Egypt	20	00
France	33	00
Germany	49	00
Greece	30	00
Hong Kong	852	001
Iceland	354	00
India	91	00
Indonesia	62	001
Iraq	964	00

For any country not listed here, visit
www.countrycallingcodes.com

COUNTRY	DIAL IN	DIAL OUT
*Ireland**	353	00
Israel	972	00
Italy	39	00
Japan	81	001
Kenya	254	000
Korea (South)	82	001
Mexico	52	00
Netherlands	31	00
New Zealand	64	00
Norway	47	00
Philippines	63	00
Portugal	351	00
Russia	7	8~10
Singapore	65	001
South Africa	27	09
Spain	34	00
Sweden	46	00
Switzerland	41	00
Taiwan	886	002
Thailand	66	001
Turkey	90	00
UK	44	00
USA	1	011

Except Northern Ireland which is part of the United Kingdom

METRIC CONVERSIONS

DISTANCE:

1 mile = 1.61 kilometers (km)

VOLUME:

1 ounce = 29.57 milliliters (ml)

8 ounces = 236.59 milliliters (ml)

1 liter (l) = 33.81 fluid ounces
              or 0.26 gallons

WEIGHT:

1 ounce = 28.35 grams (g)

1 pound = 0.45 kilograms (kg)

1 kilogram (kg) = 2.20 pounds

TEMPERATURE:

32 degrees Fahrenheit = 0 degrees Celsius

10 degrees Celsius = 50 degrees Fahrenheit

20 degrees Celsius = 68 degrees Fahrenheit

30 degrees Celsius = 86 degrees Fahrenheit